M000049557

WHAT

NOT

TO

SAY

LOVE & ROMANCE

A Compendium of the
Worst Possible Things
You Can Utter Aloud

**KNOCK
KNOCK**®
LOS ANGELES, CALIFORNIA

WHAT NOT TO SAY

CONTENTS

CONTENTS

WHAT NOT TO SAY

CONTENTS

INTRODUCTION

"Better slip with foot than tongue."

Ben Franklin had a lot to say, and he most certainly knew a thing or two about what not to say, as evidenced by this quote. Unless you've taken a vow of silence at an ashram or are pleading the Fifth in the courtroom, you're probably susceptible to putting your proverbial foot in your proverbial mouth. We've all had moments in which we've uttered thoughtless, ignorant, insensitive, tactless, entitled, or just plain bone-headed remarks.

While faux pas can be made at any time and in any place, the world of love and romance encompasses many high-risk, emotionally fraught situations. Not only does the quality of our daily life revolve around successfully completing these one-on-one romantic interactions, our very happiness depends on effective communication with those we hold dear, those we dearly want to hold, or those we want to keep at arm's length.

That's where this book comes to the rescue. It's a handy reference guide for what to avoid saying in situations ranging from a first date to breaking up to being caught cheating to proposing marriage; a cheat sheet of no-go remarks when talking to people like your husband, your wife, a stripper, or your in-laws.

For instance, when talking to a partner who has just discovered she is pregnant, "Is it mine?" is a recipe for disaster. It's also probably best to avoid anything like "Yes, those pants do make you look fat" during an argument. And never tell a man "Wow, your hands are so small!" Chances are you'll end up having to consult this book for what not to say when getting dumped.

Verbal gaffes are just one component of this book. In addition to a list of specific phrases that you should avoid, there are helpful sidebars with tips, tricks, and cautionary tales. And featured throughout the book are ten things one should never, ever, verbalize in a relationship under any circumstances—a veritable Hall of Fame of what not to say.

While some people have the amazing capacity to utter completely dunderheaded remarks and never pay the price, most of us are not so lucky. As turn-of-the-century horticulturalist and noted conversationalist Lady Dorothy Nevill remarked, "The real art of conversation is not only to say the right thing at the right place but to leave unsaid the wrong thing at the tempting moment." Or, as this quote attributed to Abraham Lincoln says, "Better to remain silent and be thought a fool than to speak out and remove all doubt."

WHAT NOT TO SAY IN
A RELATIONSHIP, EVER

I wish
I'd never
met you.

AFFAIR

<u>1</u> I wanted to get a Porsche for my midlife crisis, but we didn't have the money.

<u>2</u> He used emojis in a way I've never experienced.

<u>3</u> The irony is that I don't even like her.

<u>4</u> I'm practicing for you.

<u>5</u> By the time I realized Tinder wasn't about campfires, it was too late.

<u>6</u> He doesn't mean anything to me.

<u>7</u> This must really suck for you.

<u>8</u> Want to join?

<u>9</u> He rang me up for coffee and things got out of hand.

<u>10</u> Surprise!

WHAT NOT TO SAY WHEN

APOLOGIZING

1 I'm sorry that this is all your fault.

2 At least I didn't break any furniture.

3 Let's do that again!

4 I admire how you stood your ground even though you were wrong.

5 Promise me next time you'll just go away.

6 That's the last time I voice an honest thought.

7 At least we're great together at something—fighting.

8 Someday we'll look back on this and you'll see I was right.

9 You made good points despite your stupidity.

10 Sorry not sorry.

BREAKING UP
IS HARD TO DO

You've been there: you're enjoying yourself at dinner with the guy or gal you're dating, when they, almost casually, start listing all the things they really like about you...which leads to a giant "BUT." Like slowly pulling a super-sticky BandAid off the hairiest part of your body, breakups are incredibly painful affairs, often made worse because of all the preliminary blathering and flattery. A 2017 study published by researchers from Brigham Young University and University of South Alabama found that being direct is the best practice. So sit your soon-to-be ex down in person, say "this isn't working for me," and cut off the relationship as quickly and honestly as you can. "I'm sorry, but I'm breaking up with you." Rip that bandage off!

1. You sound just like your mother.

2. My friends said this would happen.

3. Yes, those pants make you look fat.

4. I can see by your face that this fight just got ugly.

5. This is why we're not married.

6. I never should have married you.

7. I hope this leads to make-up sex.

8. Wake me when you're done talking.

9. Your blood sugar is clearly low.

10. First, can we figure out what's for dinner?

BAD MOOD

1 Do I look fat?

2 Do you like my family?

3 Do you love me?

4 Should I cut my hair?

5 Do you think I need a therapist?

6 I still think you were wrong about that.

7 Let's talk about us.

8 Do you want to know what *else* is bothering me?

9 Give me your credit card.

10 Tequila!

1. Are you sure it's your birthday today?

2. A surprise party with your biological parents seemed like a fun idea to me.

3. You look more like your father every day.

4. You look more like your mother every day.

5. I figured since you hate getting older, you wouldn't want me to mention it.

6. Wow, you look much older than thirty-five.

7. I asked your dad what your exact bra size is to get it just right.

8. I made a romantic dinner reservation to celebrate at Dave & Buster's.

9. I bet your wish was to lose those last ten pounds.

10. But you *said* you didn't want anything!

ACTIONS
SPEAK LOUDER

If you want a successful romance, stop quoting poetry and start doing the dishes. According to a study conducted at Pennsylvania State University, which set out to learn how and when people feel loved (and how to maintain that feeling), researchers found that most people felt actions were more important than words when it comes to romantic overtures. Put quite simply, don't just *say* "I love you," but rather *show* that you love them. Of course, don't make your relationship a silent movie. Lead researcher Saeideh Heshmati said, "I think it's important to communicate these things to each other, which can assist in being more in tune with each other and feeling loved in the relationship." So, y'know, you can talk, but don't *just* talk.

BREAKING UP

1. I totally want you—to go away.

2. We can't be "friends with benefits" if there's no benefit.

3. It's not you, it's your odor.

4. Maybe we should just take a break.

5. This could've worked out if you weren't such a jackass.

6. I need time to focus on my career.

7. I'd give you a map if it would help you find my G-spot.

8. What's the best emoji for "I hate you"?

9. I need to be free to find my soulmate.

10. I want to spend more time with my Xbox.

WHAT NOT TO SAY IN
A RELATIONSHIP, EVER

You can't
do anything
right.

CHEATING

<u>1</u> I'll get in bed in a second—I just need to shower first.

<u>2</u> Can you believe my boss scheduled another business trip?

<u>3</u> Oh, we were just joking around in those emails.

<u>4</u> The lipstick on my collar? My mother's!

<u>5</u> No, that's not men's cologne—I decided to switch fragrances.

<u>6</u> It never happened.

<u>7</u> He was trying to seduce me, but it didn't work.

<u>8</u> We're just friends.

<u>9</u> I'm not in the least bit attracted to him.

<u>10</u> I'm not in the least bit attracted to her.

WHAT NOT TO SAY WHEN DIVIDING

CHORES

1 Isn't this women's work?

2 I'll supervise.

3 You should do this for a living.

4 Mind if I get you an outfit?

5 It's just that you're so much better at this than I am.

6 You cooked, so it's your mess.

7 I'd ask for your help, but you're awful.

8 You never asked me to clean before we moved in together.

9 My last boyfriend did the dishes better.

10 Mind if I nap while you work?

1. Don't worry about the sheets. They're dirty already.

2. I don't get it—*that's* what all the fuss is about?

3. He shoots! He scores!

4. Ewwww.

5. Don't forget to vote for me.

6. Remind me to take my pants off next time.

7. I did it! I really did it! Yay!

8. Nice to meet you too.

9. Oh, so *that's* what that thing does.

10. Aaand…scene.

WHAT NOT TO SAY BEFORE

COFFEE

Can we talk about us?

What should we do today?

Did you hear what the president said?

We're out of coffee, but we have tea.

Do you know how exploited coffee plantation workers are?

You should cut down on caffeine.

Today is the first day of our bone-broth cleanse.

You should call your mother.

I got you low-fat half-and-half.

[a single word]

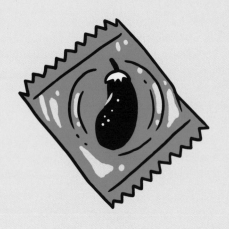

WHAT NOT TO SAY
WHEN PUTTING ON A

CONDOM

This brand is so strong, I get at least three uses out of each one!

Mind if I keep this after we're done?

After carrying this around for a year, I finally get to use it!

What's the opposite of a Magnum?

If I had a dollar for every time I did this…

I just need to say good night before I tuck the little guy in.

Roll, roll, roll the glove, gently down the peen!

Okay, so now what happens?

Are we having sex yet?

This one's got a tiny camera on it. Wait 'til you see the photos!

COUPLES COUNSELING

1. I've always had a thing for your brother.

2. Are we being billed by the hour?

3. How honest do you want me to be?

4. This is a total waste of time.

5. Do you give discounts for Yelpers?

6. I thought you said couples *massage*.

7. I'm sorry, I wasn't paying attention.

8. Women, am I right?

9. He's the one who really needs help.

10. Oral isn't cheating.

YO, BRO

Ever tease your man about how his bestie seems like his "other romance"? You might not be wrong. In the world of heterosexual relationships, dudes say bromances can be as important as romances. Professors from the UK's University of Winchester conducted a survey revealing that guys in bromances typically share secrets, are willing to feel vulnerable with their bromantic partner, and even show some marked physical affection. To be clear, all of those surveyed saw the relationship as purely nonsexual, which they claimed gave legitimacy to their female relationships. Still, it's good to know that two heterosexual dudes can hug and snuggle in a purely platonic way. Of course, that's also how literally every "coming out" story starts.

WHAT NOT TO SAY IN
A RELATIONSHIP, EVER

This is all your fault.

CRUSH

<u>1</u> . . .

<u>2</u> Want to see my handcuff collection?

<u>3</u> Someday you'll love me.

<u>4</u> Can I add you to "Find Friends"?

<u>5</u> I finally found you on Google Earth.

<u>6</u> How's your aunt's ex-son-in-law doing now?

<u>7</u> Why are your Facebook security settings so tight?

<u>8</u> You've got a great social security number.

<u>9</u> Have you ever had a stalker?

<u>10</u> Why do you smell so good?

WHAT NOT TO SAY
WHEN ASKING FOR A

DIVORCE

It's not you, it's me.

You're more in love with me than I am with you.

My mother says I deserve better.

I realized you're not "the one."

I think I might be gay.

I think I might be straight.

I used to think your idiosyncrasies were cute—now they bug me.

I'll just end up hurting you.

Have you heard of love at first sight? How about misery at five years?

There's someone else.

We can all fit if you sit on the handlebars.

My parole officer said I couldn't be alone with you.

Four separate checks, right?

We should get a polo team together.

Oh, no. My date is deflating.

We can swap after dinner.

Thanks for driving, Mom.

So this is how group sex starts.

Which one of you wants to go first?

This is exactly how my years in that cult started.

<u>1</u> Is your refrigerator running?

<u>2</u> Mommy?

<u>3</u> I love you.

<u>4</u> I want your babies.

<u>5</u> Guess how many drinks I've had.

<u>6</u> I think I'm going to barf.

<u>7</u> Are you DTF?

<u>8</u> Why don't you love me?

<u>9</u> LOVE ME!

<u>10</u> [anything at all]

Women—do you ever long for verbal reassurance from your man and not get it? Here's an easier way to feel less anxious: smelling your boyfriend can reduce stress for women in a heterosexual relationship. That's according to a University of British Columbia study in which researchers had males in a relationship wear a shirt for a day, then put the women in mock stressful situations. When given their boyfriend's shirt to smell, women experienced lower stress levels, while the opposite was true when smelling a stranger's shirt. This doesn't mean you should carry dirty laundry around with you, but it does highlight how the sense of smell can be a form of communication, much the way your coworker communicates that they had a burrito for lunch.

MONEY CAN'T
BUY YOU LOVE

Being rich might solve a lot of problems, but it can create them when it comes to relationships. *TIME* magazine collected data from various studies, and found less-affluent people demonstrated better reasoning while those with tons of money made poorer decisions. In one study, this applied specifically to interpersonal relationships, which suffered because wealthy people typically find joy in other places, such as at work. Igor Grossman, University of Waterloo associate professor of psychology, told *TIME* that rich people tend to "have less of the affordances that teach them—or force them—to reason wisely about interpersonal conflicts." So you may stress about how to pay the bills, but at least you're better at making a relationship work than ol' Mr. Moneybags.

DUMPED

1. I'm going to tell your mom.

2. My family hates you anyway.

3. You'll come crawling back.

4. I'm posting those photos.

5. You can't live without me.

6. No, I'm dumping you.

7. I was always faking it.

8. Tell me—what's wrong with me?

9. I know your credit card numbers.

10. Hallelujah!

EX IS GETTING MARRIED

1. Good luck! You'll need it.

2. Call me if you get sick of each other.

3. I hope you're into kink.

4. Have you seen her mole?

5. Maybe you can fix him.

6. What does she see in you?

7. I guess he doesn't have a type.

8. I give it six months.

9. You look just like his mother.

10. You look just like her father.

WHAT NOT TO SAY IN
A RELATIONSHIP, EVER

You've
really let
yourself go.

EXCLUSIVE

<u>1</u> I promise to start every sentence with "Hey, Pookums."

<u>2</u> Your extra room will be a great place for my Toby jug collection.

<u>3</u> I guess I can finally delete Grindr.

<u>4</u> Let me break up with my other lover first.

<u>5</u> I can't wait to tell my mother. She's in the car.

<u>6</u> The last time I took this step, it ended in a restraining order.

<u>7</u> And my dog said this would never work.

<u>8</u> So I can stop stalking you now?

<u>9</u> I'm excited about the "'til death do us part" idea.

<u>10</u> Now can you tell me where babies come from?

WHAT NOT TO SAY ON

FACEBOOK

I feel a lot closer to you now that I can follow your every move.

Your news feed appeals to the rabid, angry conspiracy theorist in me.

Here's a bit of fake news…I hate you.

I had a crush on you since high school, even though the court order kept me at least 200 feet away from campus.

You look nothing like your profile pic.

I'm just here, waiting patiently for your relationship status to change, and then I'll pounce!

Got any more photos of you with your cute friends?

I just borrowed that puppy for the photo op.

Mind if I give you a poke?

"Like" is just the start of what I want to do to you.

FALLING IN LOVE

1. I hope this doesn't end in an arrest.

2. Now we can pop each other's zits.

3. I should tell you I'm really into pudding.

4. Prepare for a few hundred texts a day.

5. I made you a copy of the key to my taxidermy shed.

6. You smell like freshly washed floor mats.

7. I like "Monty" for our baby's name.

8. I can't wait to poop with the bathroom door open.

9. I already got your name tattooed on my back.

10. What should we fight about?

If the eggplant is at the top of your list of most used emojis, you might want to reconsider how you text your girlfriend. And, hey, if you and your significant other have similar texting habits, you have a better chance of romantic success than most. So says a study conducted by psychologists at New York's Pace University that showed young people benefit from partnering with someone who shares their texting habits. For example, if you and your boo can have a whole conversation using only transportation emojis, you're one step ahead of the guy who sends his wife super funny cat gifs to which she never responds. Seriously, Alice! Did you see that cat falling off of the couch? Why don't you reply?!

WHAT NOT TO SAY
WHEN DESCRIBING A

FANTASY

You haven't eaten anything lately, have you?

…and then your mom walks in.

Do you have a paintbrush I could use?

So I'm in the bathroom at this Mexican restaurant…

This would have been before I met your mother.

Normally, I'm not attracted to animals.

You've seen *Sesame Street*, right?

It's hard for me to describe the smell.

You're there—just much, much younger.

Not a hard cheese like Parmesan, but more like a Brie.

1 You look just like my ex.

2 Does this look infected to you?

3 My parents said I could stay out past ten.

4 Is it okay if I bring my kid?

5 You're paying, right?

6 It's nice to finally be around other human beings again

7 Did you fart?

8 That wasn't a recent photo of you at all.

9 I figured we could hit the strip club after this.

10 So how many people have you slept with?

Monogamy is totally romantic—until you realize it's only been around for about a thousand years and can lead to an earlier death. Citing demographic information, research, and professional experience, psychologist Bella DePaulo wrote in an article for CNN.com that the long-held belief that marriage is good for you is largely hogwash. She said the lives of unmarried folks "are often healthier and more fulfilling than those of their coupled counterparts." According to her research, there are currently more single people than at any time in recent history and they don't consider getting married a necessary step toward adulthood. Plus, they're having way more sex than married folks. So if you haven't walked down the aisle, consider that a bullet dodged.

So you're the ones who are such bad influences.

Tell me everything about the exes.

Oh, I thought you were gay.

Next time you all go out, you'd better invite me too.

Which one of you is the pussy-whipped one?

Which one of you is the frigid one?

Wow, she never told me you were this hot!

Promise you'll tell me if he cheats.

She better not even look at someone else when she's with you.

Can I have all your phone numbers and email addresses, please?

WHAT NOT TO SAY IN
A RELATIONSHIP, EVER

It's all in
your head.

WHAT NOT TO SAY
WHEN RECEIVING A

GIFT

1 What is it?

2 Did we have a spending limit I didn't know about?

3 This is for *me*?

4 You *really* shouldn't have.

5 Do you have the receipt?

6 That's an interesting color.

7 My mom would love this.

8 Weird!

9 I saw these at the Dollar Store.

10 I suppose I can always use two.

WHAT NOT TO SAY DURING THE

HOLIDAYS

I'm thankful we only have to do this once a year.

Moist turkey meat is overrated anyway.

Can this conversation wait 'til the Epiphany?

My New Year's resolution is to stop indulging in giving oral sex.

No, it's not my job—I just like dressing as Santa.

Can the elf on the shelf watch us tonight?

My cologne is mistletoe scented, FYI.

All I want for Christmas is a prenup.

You should wear red and green more often. It's slimming.

I would have preferred coal.

1. Is that what you're wearing?

2. You would if you really loved me.

3. Aren't you a little old for that?

4. I've trained you well.

5. My mother warned me about you.

6. If I've told you once, I've told you a thousand times..

7. Where do you wanna go for dinner?

8. Which of my friends do you think is the hottest?

9. You want me to do what to you?

10. Does this make me look fat?

1. My wife is nowhere near as trashy as you.

2. Oops—I forgot my husband is coming home early today.

3. Wow, you've made a really huge mistake.

4. We're like Romeo and Juliet, except we make even worse decisions.

5. I don't care what everyone says, you're not a hussy.

6. I accidentally posted that photo of us on Instagram and Facebook and Twitter and Tumblr.

7. With all of this sneaking around, you'd think the sex would be better.

8. Did I get the clap from you or was that someone else?

9. Call me Ishmael.

10. Do you have a rabbit and a boiling pot at home?

YOU DON'T BRING ME FLOWERS ANYMORE

If nothing says "I love you" like a diamond, nothing says "I'm a nut job" like a ring made out of your tooth. But you can get one from Polly Van Der Glas, an Australian jewelry maker. It's just one of many gifts you can give your sweetheart—if you want the gift to go over very badly. Pick up a pair of his and hers tongue scrapers. How about a calendar for recording the daily state of your love life? To really knock them out, have the Bronx Zoo name a cockroach after them, or make beef jerky undies ("brief jerky"). Sure, a diamond is forever, but these gifts are unique—and think of the money you'll save. Especially after you're single again.

IN-LAWS

I love him more than you do.

Do you know why she's so uptight?

We think polyamory is an intriguing idea.

Is that the guy she lost her virginity to?

Can you believe he was still a virgin when we met?

My first in-laws were a lot richer.

It's almost as good as my mom's food.

Do you have decent long-term-care insurance?

So, how much is in the will?

She's an animal in bed.

IN THE MOOD

1. It'll only take a minute.

2. Nobody can hear us.

3. If you won't, I'll find someone who will.

4. Jesus would want you to.

5. Relax and enjoy it.

6. I just want to express my love for you.

7. I bought you flowers.

8. I know you're tired—I'll be fast.

9. I already took the Viagra!

10. Pleasepleasepleasepleaseplease.

WHAT NOT TO SAY IN
A RELATIONSHIP, EVER

Don't
take this
personally.

JILTED

1. I saw that coming a mile away.

2. You should never have been a couple in the first place

3. You guys had no chemistry.

4. I never knew what you saw in her.

5. Finally!

6. You'll make a better choice next time.

7. He can do better.

8. Maybe now you'll have more time for me.

9. Can I hit on her now that she's single?

10. Getting dumped is a great diet.

Can you create a retroactive prenup?

Wait—which husband is this for again?

Buying a Maserati last week was a necessary business expense.

I think we should file for an annulment because, frankly, the sex was terrible.

You don't mind if I forge my spouse's signature, right?

I'm a profeminist guy—I know a woman doesn't need a man to support her.

The checks I wrote to Destini and Cristal were for research assistance.

Do you want to know about all my hidden accounts?

I deserve that ten grand a month—it's the style to which I've become accustomed.

If I sleep with you, will you represent me for free?

1 How about we try a size bigger?

2 Maybe if the salesgirl tried them on?

3 I'm just browsing for my mother.

4 I can return this thong, right?

5 Are these edible?

6 Where are the granny panties?

7 What's your employee discount?

8 Do you have these in a crotchless option?

9 I'm hungry. Are you hungry?

10 Those are like the ones I saw at the strip club.

SECRET ADMIRER
OR STALKER?

You've got a crush on a cutie and you're too shy to make the move? Thinking of playing secret admirer to test the waters? Tread carefully—there's a fine line between secret admirer and stalker. If you don't want to look like a stalker, here are a few things to avoid. Don't haunt their social media, commenting, liking, and retweeting everything. Don't cozy up to their friends to pump them for information, and don't Google-research every detail of their life. Don't invade their physical or emotional space. Don't send anonymous gifts. Don't sext. Don't stand outside their house blasting a favorite love song from a boombox (well, maybe that one is okay). The best strategy when you like someone? Show a little courage and just ask them out for coffee. And take "No" for an answer.

1. The voices in my head say we should definitely do this

2. My therapist says we should definitely do this.

3. You're not going to suggest something stupid, are you?

4. We don't have to go with your choice again, do we?

5. My way, or the highway.

6. Let's ask my mother.

7. You have no idea what I like.

8. Maybe this time, you'll have a good idea.

9. I don't know—what do you want to do?

10. This is harder than Sophie's Choice.

1. You look great for your age.

2. Don't be such a baby.

3. Wow, your hands are so small!

4. Why don't you grow a pair?

5. Getting a little thin on top, aren't you?

6. You have such a nice face.

7. That's so immature.

8. Be a man!

9. I really hate your mother.

10. You're just not living up to your potential.

What do you mean, you aren't paying?

I can see your man boobs.

You aren't defined by your job.

Men aren't supposed to cry.

It must be hard to stay home while your wife works.

What—are you on your period?

I'm so much taller than you!

It's just a game.

You're such a mama's boy.

Men!

WHAT NOT TO SAY WHILE GETTING

MARRIED

I mean, look at that rack—do you blame me?

I'd like to take a few minutes of this ceremony to tell you all about my former boyfriends.

Has anyone seen the rings?

After breaking up with her sister, I thought she was the next best thing.

Seventh's time's a charm, right?

I'd like to thank my future in-laws for that future inheritance.

I'd like to thank Candi, Bambi, and Destini for last night.

I do?

Wait—gimme a minute here.

I don't.

WHAT NOT TO SAY IN
A RELATIONSHIP, EVER

You
always…

WHAT NOT TO SAY DURING A

MÉNAGE À TROIS

1. Nobody's ignoring you—the two of us are just in the pre-trois part of the evening.

2. Oh, my god, this is happening. Whoo-hoo!!

3. Eeeny meeny miney mo…

4. I'm not sure who I like more.

5. I'll get back to you as soon as I possibly can.

6. Mind if I order a pizza?

7. You get an orgasm! And you get an orgasm! And you get an orgasm!

8. I've run out of positions.

9. Cramp!

10. I'm bored.

History gives us excellent relationship role models, like Queen Victoria and Prince Albert, and Pierre and Marie Curie. It also gives us plenty of bad ones, showing us how *not* to conduct your love life. Henry the VIII agreed to marry Anne of Cleaves based on seeing her portrait, but he found her too ugly in person and had the marriage annulled. Alma Mahler broke up with her lover Oskar Kokoschka, so he had a doll maker create a life-size replica of her. And finally, stay away from anything like this extreme example of what not to say when you split with your wife: When Colonial-era businessman Timothy Dexter's marriage went south, he told people his wife died, and when they saw her, he claimed she was a ghost.

MOVING IN TOGETHER

1. I'm pretty broke, so this seems like a good idea.

2. It's cool if I pay my half of the rent in bitcoin, right?

3. I wouldn't go in the bathroom for a while.

4. I used the last of your milk this morning—I hate black coffee!

5. So that's what you look like when you wake up— every morning?

6. I found this sofa in the alley!

7. I don't know about you, but my mom does my laund

8. Now that we're together, no need for the fancy linger anymore!

9. I'm thinking about starting a new business—breedin ferrets at home.

10. My friends can still crash here when they're wasted, right?

I have a headache.

I ate too much for dinner.

I had a hard day at work.

I'm tired.

I'm sleeping.

Maybe later.

I can't—I have the song from *Sesame Street* stuck in my head.

Try me again in the morning.

I'll be there in a minute.

I was in the mood—yesterday.

TINDER MERCIES

It could be said that what happens on Tinder stays on Tinder. Unfortunately, when you don't keep track of your contacts' last names, that aphorism tends to fall by the wayside. One unlucky user started chatting with a match named Ryan, who was good-looking, nice enough, but the chemistry just wasn't there. Four months later, our heroine met another Ryan at a house party, and the sparks flew. So, she texted him to meet up again IRL. However, she didn't enter Ryan Number 2's last name into her phone. When the two met for dinner, it turned out that she had invited Tinder Ryan and not Party Ryan. Long story short, it was the most awkward dinner of her life, and an object lesson in paying closer attention to detail.

WHAT NOT TO SAY AFTER A

ONE-NIGHT STAND

Wow, I must have been SO drunk!

What did you say your name was?

This is why I'm always running out of condoms.

I can't wait to tell my mom about this.

Thanks for coming by—here's a gift basket.

You may want to get a herpes test.

You don't need a ride home, right?

A positive Yelp review would be most appreciated.

What would Jesus do now?

I love you!

<u>1</u> My divorce is almost final.

<u>2</u> Seeking someone with low standards.

<u>3</u> Nice guys don't always finish last. I finish first.

<u>4</u> Do you like puppets as much as I do?

<u>5</u> I enjoy the soothing sounds of the bowling alley.

<u>6</u> Turn-ons: chicken gravy.

<u>7</u> I'm not afraid to cry, and I do so after sex. Sometimes during.

<u>8</u> My ex called me clingy, but I like to think of myself as attentive.

<u>9</u> Occupation: youth pastor.

<u>10</u> My mom says I'm quite a catch.

They say that the honeymoon period of a relationship lasts anywhere from six months to a year. After this time, a couple really gets to know each other, and the subject of marriage can be realistically broached. But one zealous young lady across the pond was confident enough in her two-week-old relationship that she decided to propose at a leap-year party while her bestie recorded it. The girl got down on a knee, presented the family heirloom ring, and waited as his bros cheered on their boy to answer. He gently took her in his arms, lifted her up from the floor, and whispered something in her ear. Throwing the ring on the floor and storming out, the camera was left on its side to record the party as the revelers returned to celebrating. Maybe wait a little longer next time?

WHAT NOT TO SAY
WHEN MEETING YOUR PARTNER'S

PARENTS

1 So *you're* who he complains about all the time.

2 Tell me about the basement we'll be moving into.

3 Are you sure you're not the *grand*parents?

4 It's so nice to put a face to the psychology bills.

5 Would you like some cocaine?

6 I feel like "employment" is an outdated concept.

7 These are our dogs, but you can consider them your grandchildren.

8 My meds are wearing off.

9 My parents couldn't be here because they're in jail.

10 Are we in your will?

WHAT NOT TO SAY IN
A RELATIONSHIP, EVER

You
never...

1 Did you make him this way?

2 Do you want her back?

3 Why didn't you teach him to put the seat down?

4 I've almost fixed all of your damage.

5 How did you stand her mother?

6 Your loss!

7 Do you like it when she does that thing in bed?

8 I taught him how to finally love.

9 Boy, did your house need redecorating.

10 Oh, I recognize you from the sex tape.

PHONE

1 Three-way isn't just for calling, you know.

2 I was hoping you wouldn't pick up.

3 I've been told I'm pretty good at phone sex.

4 You sound tired.

5 Hurry up!

6 Call me, maybe.

7 What now?

8 Are you sitting down?

9 I'm breaking up with you.

Is that a banana in your pocket? Because I'm allergic to them.

I put the STUD in STD—all I need is U.

My dolls would love to meet you.

Want to come back to my place? My mom's away.

Do you love macramé as much as I do?

I make a great ex-boyfriend.

We should go if we're going to catch the last bus.

My love will give you a burning sensation.

Does this rag smell like chloroform to you?

I'm a pretty skilled dick-pic photographer.

When F. Scott Fitzgerald, at the time a penniless unknown writer, courted Zelda Sayre, a wealthy southern heiress, she taunted him with threats of giving in to numerous richer suitors. But when his first novel, *This Side of Paradise*, was published to wide acclaim, she enthusiastically gave in. The ensuing romance was one of infamous passion, tumult, and naked dancing in fountains that would come to be the stuff of Jazz Age legend. But during the Great Depression when money got tight and the booze ran out, the Fitzgeralds got at each other's throats. The final nail in the coffin was the fact that both had been working in secret on novels based on their terrible relationship. In the end she died in a hospital fire and he in drunken Hollywood obscurity. At least he never lived to see the latest *The Great Gatsby* remake.

1. What's that smell?

2. You voted for that idiot?

3. Pass me the tweezers.

4. That reminds me of a funny story about my mother.

5. Do you wash your sheets?

6. What do you think of the Arab/Israeli conflict?

7. Was that it?

8. Do you think we made a baby?

9. If you loved me, you would.

10. Have you accepted Jesus as your personal savior?

PREGNANT

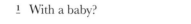

1. With a baby?

2. Is it mine?

3. Shit.

4. How did this happen?!

5. Deliberately?

6. That explains your moods!

7. Guess I should break it off with Marissa…

8. Again?!

9. Hang on, I have to call my therapist.

10. Noooooooooooooooooooo!

A man's first impulse before going out on the prowl is usually to do whatever he can to prevent sweating. The usual recourse is a shower, shave, and healthy application of antiperspirant. However, counterintuitive as it might seem, this might not be the best tactic toward securing a mate. The *Journal of Neuroscience* reports that women are attracted to the scent of male sweat, specifically the sweat given off during sexual arousal. So the next time you are about to head off for a hot date, it might be a good idea to turn up the temperature on the thermostat, turn on your favorite internet smut, and pregame, so to speak. Just make sure you save a bit of motivation for the main event.

PROPOSING MARRIAGE

1. Sorry, I'm terrible with names. You are?

2. I've done this so many times I'm not nervous anymore.

3. First off, there's this prenup I'll need you to sign.

4. I love you. Now change.

5. My knees are killing me.

6. Hang on, let me get my mom on camera to coach me through this.

7. Gee, that was easy. Now I wish I had aimed higher.

8. It's just like I said to my first wife.

9. Here is a list of my demands.

10. I only have a few minutes before the warden comes back.

WHAT NOT TO SAY IN
A RELATIONSHIP, EVER

Is it in?

SEX

1. Where should I put this?

2. This isn't my first time.

3. I think I felt it.

4. They're tears of joy.

5. Should you call your doctor?

6. Here goes nothing!

7. Mom?

8. Mexican food was a bad choice.

9. It looked bigger in the picture.

10. What the hell is *that*?

WHAT NOT TO SAY IN A

SEX SHOP

1 My grandma shops here.

2 Where is your religion section?

3 This brings back memories.

4 I'd like to rent a personal massager.

5 What's the best dildo to bring on a driving test?

6 I haven't seen this much naughty stuff since Catholic school.

7 I'm just here to people watch.

8 If you guys sold peanut butter, this would be my one-stop shop.

9 I'd like the same brand of edible underwear Margaret Thatcher had.

10 Can I also use these oils for cooking?

1. Ignore the guy in the background.

2. Ignore the girl in the background.

3. Ignore my mom in the background.

4. Ignore the sheep in the background.

5. Anthony Weiner's got nothing on me!

6. Please note the ruler I've helpfully placed nearby.

7. I'm a grower, not a shower.

8. Those spots are normal.

9. Apologies if you've already seen my pics on Pornhub.

10. TBH I've gained a little weight since then.

SLEEP TOGETHER

1. You've been tested, right?

2. Do you sleep with all your dates?

3. I knew I'd get you eventually.

4. You know I'm not ready for a relationship, right?

5. I gotta go.

6. You gotta go.

7. Please don't tell your friends.

8. Don't worry, I won't tell anyone.

9. Um, you should get checked for sleep apnea.

10. You didn't strike me as the type who would do this.

PRE-REJECTED

Beware of what you say when you are filling out an online dating profile. In some cases, prospective members are being rejected before ever joining up. Citing secret, proprietary compatibility algorithms, online dating behemoth eHarmony denies 20 percent of its applicants (including any gay candidates). At the end of an extensive survey, you're either welcomed into a pool of tens of millions or you receive this response: "Participants must fall within certain defined profiles…we regret our inability to provide service for you." In 2009, eHarmony did create a separate service for same-sex matching in a settlement of a 2005 complaint that the company's failure to offer such a service was discriminatory. Progress?

It may be that bringing up the topic of a prenup is number one on the romance list of what not to say. But hey—hope for the best, prepare for the worst. Know the law, just in case you are anxious about entering into a financially lopsided arrangement. Only 5 to 10 percent of couples actually sign one, but sometimes formalizing the details is worth the fuss. When Steven Spielberg divorced Amy Irving without having filed any precautionary paperwork, for instance, she ended up with a cool $100 million. On the other hand, she probably earned it.

You remind me of my sister.

How much of my kid's college fund will it cost for a lap dance?

I see you've been sampling the buffet.

You're going to catch a cold dressed like that.

I know you from stalking you on Facebook.

I'm just here for the music.

So where did you go to stripper school?

That looks like good cardio.

I'm no expert, but I'm pretty sure you're not an actual cowgirl.

Mind if try the pole?

What's with all of the ugly people?

I thought this was a church event.

My herpes is in remission.

I'm meeting my brother here.

How many STDs would you consider too many?

Want to go to Arby's after this?

This is how my grandparents met.

Will there be snacks?

I'm sooooo going to Snapchat this.

I'm pretty sure I won't cry this time.

WHAT NOT TO SAY IN
A RELATIONSHIP, EVER

I told you so!

1. U up?

2. Wait—who's this?

3. Send nudes.

4. Who's horny?

5. Happy Belated Anniversary!

6. Is this Beth or Susie?

7. Is this Bill or Doug?

8. You're not normally my type, but I had a great time.

9. I think I'm pregnant.

10. I'm breaking up with you.

WHAT NOT TO SAY WHEN

TOASTING THE BRIDE AND GROOM

1. Are you *sure* you want to do this?

2. For those who were wondering—yes! The baby should be here in about seven months!

3. You two are so cheap, this is the first meal with you I didn't pay for.

4. This is so crazy—we all used to think you were gay!

5. *How* many times have you been married?

6. I'm so inspired, I'd like to propose—to MY girlfriend!

7. We used to take bets on how many guys she'd hooked up with.

8. At last—someone whose self-esteem is as low as yours.

9. I'm sorry I bagged her first!

10. Hey, if it's any consolation, I didn't think he was that good in bed.

TRIP TOGETHER

1. Have you ever read a map before?

2. Clearly, you packed your attitude.

3. I'm going to need extra vomit bags.

4. I should make the schedule since you're late for everything.

5. If I fall asleep on your shoulder, be warned that I'm a drooler.

6. Let's see if I'm finally off that no-fly list.

7. I made a polka playlist for the trip.

8. When we get to the customs agent, I'm going to make a run for it.

9. When I fly, I like to watch plane-crash movies.

10. Think my steamer trunk will fit in the overhead bin?

WHAT NOT TO SAY ON

VALENTINE'S DAY

1. It's just a stupid Hallmark invention.

2. You've got me, why do you need a gift?

3. Happy Valentine's Day [points to genitals].

4. This wasn't on my list.

5. I'll take a cash gift.

6. Netflix and chill?

7. This had better be nicer than my Christmas present.

8. I didn't want to get you something fattening.

9. Let me shoot you with my Cupid arrow.

10. But it's a really high-quality Crock-Pot.

EXCUSES, EXCUSES

As Aaron Ben, Ph.D., writes in *Psychology Today*, humans get way too elaborate when rationalizing infidelity. We pose as altruists ("Without this affair, I would have left my spouse"), or diminish our guilt ("It's not my fault, it's my crazy hormones") or feelings ("It's just sex"). But cheaters, take heed. The author warns: "When you have a very good justification, one reason is usually enough; when there is no such justification, one needs to accumulate sufficient excuses as no one of them is likely to be convincing." So do yourself a favor—if you are going to offer an excuse, stop at one. Any more will sound ridiculous.

<u>1</u> You're starting to remind me of your mother.

<u>2</u> They don't make you look *that* fat.

<u>3</u> Sure, I was looking at her, but I was thinking about you

<u>4</u> Why don't you get my mother's recipe for that?

<u>5</u> It was only sex—it didn't mean anything.

<u>6</u> Are you having your period?

<u>7</u> I wanted to get you something practical.

<u>8</u> What did you *do* all day?

<u>9</u> Don't you already have enough shoes?

<u>10</u> Your sister is looking *good*!

WEDDING

1. This is the same DJ from the bride's last wedding.

2. Statistically, this marriage will probably end in divorce.

3. Is there an open bar?

4. She's not allowed to wear white.

5. I hope the wedding favors are better than last time.

6. They're probably getting married for their taxes.

7. Wow, the bride doesn't look pregnant at all.

8. I'm here to offer my services. I'm a marriage counselor.

9. Who knew cousins could find love like this?

10. I hope they play "Electric Slide."

1. You look great for your age.

2. Must be that time of the month.

3. You're a big one, aren't you?

4. You think everything is about you.

5. You have such a pretty face.

6. You've got quite the appetite for a woman.

7. When's the baby due?

8. That's pretty good—for a girl.

9. Smile!

10. You look fat when you cry.

How many guys have you slept with?

Are those real?

You'd be so much happier with a man.

You look tired.

Look who has daddy issues!

Have you gained weight?

What's your natural hair color?

When are you going to have children?

You're too sensitive.

Women!

Created, published, and distributed by Knock Knock
6080 Center Drive
Los Angeles, CA 90045
knockknockstuff.com
Knock Knock is a registered trademark of Knock Knock LLC

Illustrations by Laurène Boglio

This book is meant solely for entertainment purposes. In no event will
Knock Knock be liable to any reader for any harm, injury, or dam-
ages, including direct, indirect, incidental, special, consequential, or
punitive arising out of or in connection with the use of the information contained in this book. So there.

ISBN: 978-168349125-5
UPC: 825703-50302-9

10 9 8 7 6 5 4 3 2 1